Donating Organs in Boxes

poems by

David Walker

Finishing Line Press
Georgetown, Kentucky

Donating Organs in Boxes

Copyright © 2016 by David Walker
ISBN 978-1-63534-040-2 First Edition
All rights reserved under International and Pan-American Copyright Conventions.
No part of this book may be reproduced in any manner whatsoever without written permission from the publisher, except in the case of brief quotations embodied in critical articles and reviews.

ACKNOWLEDGMENTS

The following poems have appeared, sometimes in slightly different form, in the following magazines:

"Relativity" in *MadHat*
"Before You Fall Asleep" in *Emerge Literary Journal*
"Fable" and "Same Roofs" in *Mouse Tales Press*
"Questions I Can't Answer" in *Buck Off Magazine*
"Putting Shebah Down" in *Stoneboat*
"Creation Myth" in *Noctua Review*
"Visiting My Grandmother" and "Remodeling the Kitchen" in *Fresh Ink*
"Milk Duds" in *Misfit's Miscellany*
 "A Discussion of Religion with My Father" in *The Quotable*

David also thanks his family: Caitlin, Mikey, Pam, David M. W., Pam N., Michael, Adrienne, Joe, and Brittany for putting up with his obnoxious sense of humor and constant need for validation. Thanks are also due to his friends and mentors: Ryan, Brett, Jeff H., Chris, Brent, Leah, Michael F., Stephen, Joyce, Jeff M., Robin, Vivian, and Tim for inside jokes and red pens. And thank you to everyone that David's ever-deteriorating mind has caused him to neglect for the various reasons that you've enriched his life.

Publisher: Leah Maines
Editor: Christen Kincaid
Cover Art: Caitlin Walker and Brittany Norton
Author Photo: Caitlin Walker and Brittany Norton
Cover Design: Elizabeth Maines

Printed in the USA on acid-free paper.
Order online: www.finishinglinepress.com
also available on amazon.com

Author inquiries and mail orders:
Finishing Line Press
P. O. Box 1626
Georgetown, Kentucky 40324
U. S. A.

Table of Contents

Relativity 1
Love Co. 2
The Pickup 3
Before You Fall Asleep 4
Fable 5
Courtship 6
Questions I Can't Answer 8
Putting Shebah Down 10
Creation Myth 12
You once said 13
boxes 14
Visiting My Grandmother 15
Remodeling the Kitchen 17
The Kiss at the End of the World 18
Same Roofs 20
The Problem with Vegetables 21
Milk Duds 22
The Things I Should Have Said to Kill Time at the
    DMV Instead of "God, It's Been a Mild Winter" 23
A Discussion of Religion with My Father 25

For the bench across from Parenzo

Relativity

If I was to throw a ball at thirty mph
next to a man running at forty mph
then it would appear that the ball was
traveling backwards. To the man,
of course. To me it would appear as if
I was in the presence of an abnormally
fast man and that I need to hit the gym.
The man would probably share my
assessment on both accounts although
we would still perceive the ball differently.
The direction of travel, not the fact
that I have a pretty shitty arm and that
the ball was moving abnormally slow.
Although how could he really tell
considering the fact that he was moving
abnormally fast? Could I really consider
him a reliable judge of velocity?

Because,
say I wrote you a letter, folded it into
a paper airplane, and had someone with
a slightly better arm than me send it flying
at forty mph. The man would perceive
the letter as static. Both the man and the letter
would arrive on your doorstep at 6:01 EST
with the sun setting in the distance. To me
the sun would appear to be at its highest
point. The ink would have run leaving
the message unreadable. You would
quickly realize that I was the only person
with whom you still communicated through
letters. You would email me your reply
forgetting that I don't own a computer.
I would write you more love letters
forgetting you don't care for romance.
The abnormally fast man would finally
stop running remembering he forgot
milk on the way home.

Love Co.

Every moment with you is translated into a monetary value that is determined in accordance with labor legislation by the Commonwealth of Massachusetts. I am compensated (on a semi-regular basis) based on the number of romantic comedies I view with you, the ratio of foot massages given and received, the average time (in seconds) of maintained eye contact after an attractive female passes, and the accuracy of summary in response to the question, "Were you even listening to me?" Each outing to the movies must be thoroughly documented on a blank CF-19 form, including a detailed analysis and plot summary of the film and a comprehensive list of concessional related purchases (non-refundable.)

After my most recent self-evaluation, in which I wrote, "I feel as though I show great promise here. I display a high level of dedication, am regularly improving my conflict-resolution abilities, and am borderline smitten with my duties," you asked what I believed the cultivating factors for my conflict-resolution abilities are, suggested that I think carefully before answering, and wondered if I might not want to amend or remove entirely the word "borderline."

The Pickup

My dad is pushing me over the fence,
his palms on the soles of my shoes,
a chain-link fence between the street
and a field with patched grass and a rusted
hubcap. We both see the faded lacquered
poles marking the edges of the backstop,
the in-between blown away like
dandelion seeds over the years.

His fist pats the webbing of his glove; dirt
coughs out in a cloud and he bends
to pick up the ball. I waver an aluminum
bat over my head as he forms a fastball, fingers
on the stitching, looks in, he's in the stretch,
holds the runner, the pitch!

My bat connects—the Sox faithful
are on their feet, the Monster
puffs out its chest, bracing, but the ball soars
over and craters Lansdowne. My dad twirls
a finger in the air and I sprint clumsily
around the best diamond I can make before
sliding back home. He jogs away to retrieve
the ball from the thicket, surely lost.

I drag the bat behind
me and we load into the pickup.
I plead with him until he finally brakes.
He lets me out and hoists me into the truck's bed.
I watch fresh lawns and folk art mailboxes
whizz by until we turn onto our street.
It feels like we are dragging
the wind, letting it coil behind us like rope.

Before You Fall Asleep

she fits perfectly into that wishbone
curve of your armpit, the television a perfect,
silent heartbeat of quivering blues pulsating
the heartbreak, betrayal, all unsaid
emotion of every person
against your wallpaper,
and you feel it all like road salt
through a boot, enough so you want
to wake her and drive to the places
she always told you she wanted to see,
the places you want to see so you can
remember the auburn setting sun
against the sea spittle on her skin,
this hemisphere's unique heat
trapped in her skin.

Fable

Before the world
had any inkling of romance or canons,
television or dinners on plastic trays,
he knew of sweat pooling
in her navel. After flight
was achieved and cold fusion
hypothesized, the poet slid chalk
across a wall passing both their initials
through a ventricle.

Now the poet writes trying to capture
something akin. But his notes to her are simply
oranges picked and hands spit-washed
from sticky juice. No one eats letters
and tastes the fruit it spells out.

A few minutes after the very first origami
crane was folded, he desperately carved a final line
to her into rock before slamming
his fist down, unsatisfied, splitting Pangaea.

Courtship

I.
You are the most breathtaking girl
I've ever met. That's not right.
I take the eraser and scrape the word
'girl' off the paper. I blow
away the scrapings and replace
girl with woman. Girls

don't put out. Women do. I'm sick
of being the quiet observer in the locker room,
just nodding and smiling away when
my teammates start talking sex. The
words 'tight' and 'wet' swaggering
from their mouths with members-

only inflection. It's more than I can
bear. I just need the thing done. I'm
caught up in the math of sex—the average
length of time in minutes it takes a woman
to climax, the number of people who
lose their virginity before fifteen,

the odds of contracting an STD
without a condom. I know that
Lorraine has had seven boyfriends,
five reportedly slept with her, giving
me a 71% chance of getting lucky
with her—the highest odds in the school.

This is not to get off; this is survival,
a rite of passage that makes the weak
easy to spot. I will not be the lingering
antelope. They say Newton died
a virgin. I'm not planning on
splitting the atom anytime soon.

II.
We were under autumn air when I
spun her around in a waltz, dipped
her low, and kissed her forehead.
She pulled the back of my neck
to guide my lips to hers. That can
sum up the entirety of our relationship:

I lead. She leads. Together we make
beautiful music. Before I knew what
happened, we were in love. They say
it's a hard jolt, like a bump in the road
- at least my uncle does—but I found
it more like osmosis, applying sunscreen

in the car before the beach. We have
never returned the words to each other.
I said it once one day not long after
our dance. I was whipping wet spaghetti
noodles against the cabinets to see if they
stuck, and she was in the other room,

accenting each thwack with an over-
exaggerated *BOOM!* as if I were toppling
skyscrapers with flimsy pasta. I laughed
and reflexively called the words out. She
grew silent and before long she was in
the kitchen with me, explaining that we

don't need to insist, or profess, or convince
each other that we're in love. *Words just
cheapen what we feel*, she said. But I knew
better. Journal upon journal of her words
proved she respected their power. Love requires
the mandate of writers: Show, don't tell.

Questions I Can't Answer

My girlfriend asks me how I could forgive him
and I say, "He's my father."

My girlfriend says, "I don't know
if I could do that," and I say,
"I didn't think I could either, but I did."

I say that when I was thirteen my sister
and I were watching the Sox
one night and my dad came home late,

sat down, and told us that something bad happened.
He went on, said that when he was visiting

family he had found someone and that he was going
to spend his birthday with her instead of us.
My sister said, "What do you mean 'her'?"

but we both knew. I say my mother was away
for the weekend, we were left alone with my dad,
and we planned on celebrating his birthday the next day.

I say that my sister and dad
talked for awhile while I just stared
at the TV, picking out each pixel,

how it vibrated, looking scared of the millions
that surrounded it, but I don't tell my girlfriend that last
part. She says, "That's horrible," and I nod.

I say, "But I don't think one bad thing can erase
all the good he's done for me," and think
that sounds about right.

Say, "He's my father."
The songs he made out of our dog's name,
the candy bars he snuck home after Mom

said, 'No.' I say, "Now we have two
Christmases," and smile. "I barely
see him," I say and say that at least

when I see him I see him good,
not the bad too, no more eggshells,
and she says, "That's good."

I should've said, "No, it's fucked
up. A dad stays with a mom because
he loves her, he loves his two kids,

his dog and three cats. He'd miss Christmases
with the family too much to leave,"
but I didn't say that.

I just say,
"He's my father," and leave it at that.

Putting Shebah Down

Morning of, I ate breakfast:
yogurt, blueberry.

She was in my sister's
room, like a salmon, breathing,
with one eye up, the other buried
in carpet.

I knelt beside her, buried my head
in her fur, kissed her, something I hadn't done
in years. I was alone
and spoke words I won't repeat.

My dad came. So did my brother. We talked about the Pats,
that time she ran into the glass door thinking it was open,
what hospital we were bringing her to.
She was standing there, in the grass,
legs spread like an unlocked tripod.

The ride to the vet was short, just down the road,
me in the backseat gripping her collar
as she slid around in the back of the SUV trying to get a footing.
She used to stick her head out the window,
globs of saliva flapping out, sticking to the window
behind her. When it was cold, we would crank the window down
just enough and she would stick her nose
up to the opening, but now she was in the way back
and the windows didn't go down back there.

The woman behind the desk couldn't get the name right,
asked for our address, if this was the first
time we'd brought her here, then she typed away.
I cupped her ears, tried to stand
her up tall, her claws scuffing the linoleum. She was

slipping through my hands. I could see she just wanted to lie
on her side, breathe, or not. Standing made it hard
to breathe. Breathing making it hard to stand.
All I wanted was to rip the keyboard
from the wall and shout *We're just trying to kill our dog!*

Then Shebah was in the room, we all were, a doctor, syringe.
The vet put a blanket down. I told her what a good dog she'd been,
close to her ear, pulled back my hand and came up with fur. I felt guilty,
wanting to wash it off.

Creation Myth

I took the sun out of the sky and pushed its button - blew it up. Wadded the Earth up between my fingers until it was a little ball like a squished ant. Then I hurled it into nothingness. Flicked it between all the stars and twinkling comet trails. Then I took a straw and sucked up all the black in space. The dark energy, Jupiter's 16 to 27 moons, and that former-planet Pluto went down smooth. Slurped everything up until there was nothing left. Then I went to work creating a new solar system. An exact replica of the original. Not much changed except minor discoloration where I spilled my coffee next to Venus. When I was finished putting everything back in its place, I drew the paths of orbit on my Etch-A-Sketch and sent the planets back in motion. After all this, I found you and told you of the moon and the fluttering of my heart, about two star-crossed lovers from two houses alike in dignity, wrote it down and dedicated it to you. Nothing was cliché anymore. All the words from all the people who said it better than I ever could were no longer untouchable because I said it first. My words were the words that boyfriends quoted, that lovers sobbed out to end an argument. Even "I love you" in a poem became acceptable again.

You once said

clichés are just truths who have died under the scalpel
of an unskilled surgeon. It takes a true artist to revive the honesty
in those once nubile bodies.

I say, *An artist can't perform miracles.*

There are no miracles. There is a science in everything
done, a math that we have yet to calculate. I don't think
we truly understand how each cog spins just so. I don't
even think the clockmaker does.

I say, *How did he build it, then?*

You think God understands why everyone does what they
do?

I say, *That's not a question of how.*

I think you're asking the wrong questions. You're still
not getting it. Some girls want roses. They want walks
on the beach. They want chocolate and stuffed animals
no matter how progressive they are. They want to be woo'ed
and romanced and have their white knight on his shiny
damn horse ride them away into the sunset. I've never
been good at math—you know that—so I don't understand
it, but it's what I want. And you're an artist so I need you
to figure out how to bring back the dead.

boxes

(noun)
1. *a container with a flat base and sides.* My mother comes home to all your things packed away. Neat. Tidy. Calculated. Your ways.
2. *an area or space enclosed within straight lines.* I remember the first time you and I met. I thought I had you sized up in five minutes. I guess I was putting you into my own boxes, but that's the thing about packing: you always miss something.
3. *a protective casing for a piece of a mechanism.* I remember her voice coming through the phone. She repeated my name to make sure it was me. Then, *He's leaving*. I rushed home and we bought a pizza. We ate and talked about how we should have seen this coming and how you were getting drunk and how you bought a condo to move into after you told my mother you didn't love her anymore and then I crushed the pizza box and brought it out to the recycling.

(verb)
1. *restrict the ability of someone to move freely.* In the morning, I wrote you a note and left it on one of the boxes you were coming to pick up that day. It told you off: my gut reactions. I wanted it to hurt you, but it didn't. I remember helping you move in years ago. Box after box you'd eventually be carrying out yourself.

Visiting My Grandmother

Eventually we would be pulling
up to a large pill-pink building
with a crucified Jesus out front
and nuns pushing patients

around the patio in wheelchairs.
We would be shifting uncomfortably
as we rode up the elevator with an old
man in a baby blue bathrobe; our

mother holding my sister's hand
and I trying not to stare at the old
man's liver spots long enough
to connect them into a distorted

Bugs Bunny with a missing ear.
We would be hovering behind
my mother. My grandmother
would be lying on a bed with too

many blankets over her. Her
limbs would be curling
at the edges like a burnt leaf.
She would shake a hand at me

and motion to a drawer with a purse
in it. I would grab the purse
and bring it to her and she would
say something. My mother would

translate the vowels and hard
kuh-kuh-kuhs and say, "She wants
you to take five dollars." I remember
thinking: So that's the going rate

for a lifetime of memories with
a grandparent. I get drool-soaked
linens and hospital-bed pungency,
an aversion to car rides

down a certain stretch of road
in northern Connecticut.

Remodeling the Kitchen

Soon after my father moved out,
we stripped the island, painted the walls
a sickly yellow, and installed marble
countertops—something close enough
so no one could tell the difference.

Demo uncovered dust decades old;
our cousin still lived with us then,
took our hot water and eggs.
Grime from when my parents
pretended to be happy.

For weeks we got
our water from a temporary sink:
our old sink pulled from the wall
and wheeled out to the middle
of the kitchen. The hose tethered
from the wall looked like my cat's tail
caught in the sliding door. My father
had closed the door too quickly
when letting her in. Howling,
she clawed the carpet. Piss matted
her hind legs—too scared and too frantic
to let him back near her. When she
had finally worked her way free,
there was fur caught in the track
and a bald spot left on her tail
that has never grown back.

The Kiss at the End of the World

The couple kissed as if the last reserves
of oxygen were locked in each other's
bodies. Reeled closer and closer and

further like magnets shook in a cup,
poles locking and locking and repelling,
the space between determined only

by its relation to its previous state.
Outside, the mortar between bricks
was deteriorating, trees began pumping

out yellow-brown smog later determined
to be mustard gas, the strings
of the pianos in the world snapped all

at once creating an off-key thunder
boom. Inside, the couple's fingers knew
each other's creases, moles, that scar

below his ribcage, the shudder she gave
off when he tickled behind her ear,
the residue of saliva on their bottom lips

like the singe of a hot light bulb.
The final tectonic plate shattered
quick as if against a wallpapered

kitchen wall sending a wave of rubble
lumbering across all seven continents.
The survivors swapped stories of destruction

of that day, pitching taillight fragments into
the campfire forged in the middle of
I-91 past exit 42. When the group

came to the couple, they both shifted
their boots in the ash and darted their
eyes like kids embarrassed to dance at prom.

Same Roofs

Right over there, you said pointing
up the mountain at a swirling
weathervane atop a house. *That's
where I live.* We eventually wound
up ribbon-like roads and came
upon your house. For months after,
I would drip oil on that same spot.
We would lay our backs against
the cold glass of my car
and pretend we knew where Cancer
was. You would stand outside
and dance in the road so I couldn't
leave at night, breath clouds
sailing away. Sometimes I would
tap on your window to surprise
you or try to end an argument
and you would sneak me in.

Now we brush our teeth in the same sink
and remind each other to lock up.
We each have our own indents
in the same bed and we cook meals
for each other. Eggs, toast, and bacon
in the mornings, Shake 'N Bake
chicken for dinner. Nothing fancy.
You're in Florida now. The sink,
the bed, the kitchen all feel like someone
else's and I want nothing more than
to leave oil stains where you are.

The Problem with Vegetables

I have yet to master the
proper techniques of corralling garden
peas into my spoon. I shudder when
presented with the overwhelming
magnitude of corn-off-the-cob kernels.
And sure, you can try your hand at securing
a stalk of broccoli to the tines of your
fork, but more often than not you are
simply and precariously balancing your healthy
cargo from plate to mouth with shaky
inefficiency.

I guess this is why I choose junk food.
I find melting M&Ms in my palm
an easier endeavor than eating anything
from the base of the food pyramid. And now
I must figure out how to successfully accomplish
this task while also making airplane
noises? How will my newborn son
understand the importance of nutrition
if he sees his father struggling to feed
him the very food that is nutritional?
And what will he make of his overweight
father? Will he take the lack of a perfect
corn cob holder good enough reason
to not eat right? Will he always choose
the vastly easier-to-eat donut?

With four months to go, I vow to master
the mysterious art of vegetable eating
and pray you really can't split something
so small with the edge of a fork.

Milk Duds

That's what you remind me of:
a particularly stubborn fragment
in need of that expert maneuvering
of fingernail and tongue to free.
Like an itch roosted between
my first and second molar. Leaning
over a sink, my index prodding, a convulsion
that stains my saliva a chocolaty brown
before I feel you released from your perch.
I spit into porcelain, watch the rush of water
wash traces away—standing mollified
for one more savor of you.

The Things I Should Have Said to Kill Time at the DMV Instead of "God, It's Been a Mild Winter"

That I never could quite get used to the taste
of vanilla ice cream. That I always wanted
to play the saxophone and that you look
your most adorable when you're angry.

Those years in Morocco staring at the ocean
and contemplating suicide were a lie.
I should've told you the first day we met,
when the wind was blowing your skirt

dangerously high up your legs and you were
crunching leaves under your sandals, that I am
a hopeless romantic. You should know that
I am distinctly familiar with the feeling of

chicken grease between my fingers. Not
the kind that you get from eating it but
preparing it. That I have never read
Paradise Lost. That I have heard great things.

Sometimes when traveling and staring
at the ocean, I wonder what salt water
in my lungs would taste like, if it would have
a taste at all. You should know that the melting

point of wax depends on its origin
and that I have always loved you. That
my feet get cold in the summer. That I once
bowled in a league with my father and that

he spent his forty-ninth birthday with his
mistress. I should have told you that I believe
in ghosts and God and America. That
it bothered me more than it should

when you told me you didn't really care
for pizza. I know the complete life cycle
of a star and that the universe is
expanding. I hate to sweep and I see

more than blue when I look into your eyes.
I miss baseball most when I hear the leaves
crunch under your sandals. And I was scared
of commitment long after you said

"I want things to be the way they were."
I like to people watch and that I am
self-conscious of the way I tie my shoes.
I should have told you that I was scared

of bees long before I stuck my hand
in that beehive.

A Discussion of Religion with my Father

Dave, I'm worried about your soul
my father tells me. For his sake
I pretend I'm not my own man,

that I still hang on his every word,
that I'm still peering at the chocolate
bars—the counter up to my nose—

pleading *That one!* He says I need
to go to church more, asks how else will
I know the Lord? I can't say my girlfriend's

mom knew the Lord well when
she took belt and fist to her own daughter
for years. Years later I was sitting on front

porches trying to glue back
pieces of my girlfriend like shattered lamp
and every Sunday her mother would

cross her fingers from her head to her chest
to her shoulders like that holy water was an iodine
soaked dishrag, a puddle of bleach and a

squeegee. My father passes a book
across the table, *For you and your*
girlfriend. Tells you how to maintain

a loving Christian relationship. He spills
coffee on his third wedding band and jumps
up to grab a napkin. I think to myself:

Thou shall not cheat on your wife
while visiting relatives in Ohio.
I tell him I'll read the book.

David Walker was introspective from a young age. His parents often reminisce of long car rides with him in silence, only broken sporadically by the clumsily organized musings of his childlike observations. When they passed a cow grazing in a field, David would mentally dissect the heifer like a butcher—examining the stifle, dewlap, and fetlock until he could render an ill-cut chunk of meat. If he were older, they would have called him a poet. At the time, however, he was simply precocious.

David now has a precocious youngster of his own with the love of his life, Caitlin. Fatherhood has happily monopolized his time and his ultimate goal is setting good examples for his son. David's nighttime routine consists of reading *A Series of Unfortunate Events* to his oft-distracted toddler before rocking him to sleep. Poetry is in his everyday.

David currently holds an MFA in Poetry from Southern Connecticut State University. He has been a workshop leader at the Salem Poetry Seminar and the Freshwater Poetry Festival. Many of his poetry and one of his short stories appear online and in print. He has read his work at various venues across the country and is the founding editor of *Golden Walkman Magazine*, a literary magazine in the form of a podcast.

www.ingramcontent.com/pod-product-compliance
Lightning Source LLC
LaVergne TN
LVHW041515070426
835507LV00012B/1599